Instant Windows PowerShell

Manage and automate your Windows Server Environment efficiently using PowerShell

Vinith Menon

BIRMINGHAM - MUMBAI

Instant Windows PowerShell

First published: October 2013

Production Reference: 1231013

Published by Packt Publishing Ltd.

Livery Place
35 Livery Street
Birmingham B3 2PB, UK.

ISBN 978-1-84968-874-1

www.packtpub.com

Credits

Author

Vinith Menon

Reviewers

Ravikanth Chaganti

Fabrice ZERROUKI

Acquisition Editors

Akram Hussain

Gregory Wild

Commissioning Editor

Manasi Pandire

Technical Editors

Veena Pagare

Arwa Manasawala

Copy Editors

Dipti Kapadia

Adithi Shetty

Project Coordinator

Joel Goveya

Proofreader

Clyde Jenkins

Production Coordinator

Adonia Jones

Cover Work

Adonia Jones

Cover Image

Prachali Bhiwandkar

About the Author

Vinith has over six years of experience in the IT industry. At the beginning of his career, he worked with Wipro Technologies as a senior systems engineer, managing a datacenter consisting of Windows servers and VMware virtualized environment. He was also extensively involved in automation using VBScripting.

Later in his career, he worked with Accenture as a senior software engineer, managing Microsoft Hyper-V and NetApp storage environment for Avanade.

He has done automation for tasks that required manual work using System Center Orchestrator and integrated them with PowerShell to deliver outstanding automation results for Avanade.

He also has experience in building Orchestrator Integration Packs using PowerShell for Microsoft System Center Orchestrator. He has extensive knowledge in Hyper-V, SCVMM, and other system center technologies. He has deep technical expertise in PowerShell scripting, Server Administration, Network Management, and Active Directory.

He is currently working as a technical marketing engineer with the Microsoft Business Unit at NetApp. He also works closely with the NetApp Engineering and Product Management team and helps in the automation of various tasks using PowerShell scripting, Microsoft Hyper-V virtualization, and System Center Technologies, such as SCSM, SCOM, and SCORCH 2012.

As a subject matter expert in Hyper-V and PowerShell, he blogs and supports the NetApp PowerShell community.

He is very passionate about automation and PowerShell scripting, and you can find him frequently blogging about virtualization, PowerShell, and automation on his personal blog, www. vinithmenon.com.

He is a Microsoft-certified IT professional and also holds a NetApp-certified Data Management Professional certification.

He has also taken sessions at the PSBUG (PowerShell Bangalore users group) about PowerShell, cloud computing, and server virtualization.

About the Reviewers

Ravikanth Chaganti has more than 12 years of experience in the IT industry. At the beginning of his career, he worked at Wipro Infotech, managing Windows, Solaris servers, and Cisco network equipment. He currently works at Dell Inc. as a lead engineer in the SharePoint solutions group. As a part of his work, he authored several white papers on MOSS 2007 and SharePoint 2010 that provide guidance on infrastructure elements of a SharePoint deployment. His work also involves performance testing and sizing of SharePoint workloads on Dell servers and storage.

He is passionate about automation and besides work, he regularly writes on his blog, `http://www.ravichaganti.com/blog`, about topics related to Windows PowerShell, Microsoft SharePoint, and Windows Server Virtualization.

In 2010, he received Microsoft's Most Valuable Professional (MVP) award for Windows PowerShell. You can also hear him speak regularly at BITPro (`http://bitpro.in`) user group meetings and other in-person events at Bangalore, India.

Fabrice ZERROUKI is a senior Microsoft consultant and has over 15 years of experience in web hosting.

He is a Microsoft technologies specialist, and is passionate about all the new and powerful technologies, as well as open source. In 2013, he received the Microsoft® Most Valuable Professional (MVP) award in Windows PowerShell Project management skills. He also holds the PRINCE2 certification (Foundation and Practitioner).

www.packtpub.com

Support files, eBooks, discount offers and more

You might want to visit www.packtpub.com for support files and downloads related to your book.

Did you know that Packt offers eBook versions of every book published, with PDF and ePub files available? You can upgrade to the eBook version at www.packtpub.com and as a print book customer, you are entitled to a discount on the eBook copy. Get in touch with us at service@packtpub.com for more details.

At www.packtpub.com, you can also read a collection of free technical articles, sign up for a range of free newsletters and receive exclusive discounts and offers on Packt books and eBooks.

packtlib.packtpub.com

Do you need instant solutions to your IT questions? PacktLib is Packt's online digital book library. Here, you can access, read and search across Packt's entire library of books.

Why Subscribe?

- ✦ Fully searchable across every book published by Packt
- ✦ Copy and paste, print and bookmark content
- ✦ On demand and accessible via web browser

Free Access for Packt account holders

If you have an account with Packt at www.packtpub.com, you can use this to access PacktLib today and view nine entirely free books. Simply use your login credentials for immediate access.

Table of Contents

Instant Windows PowerShell	**1**
So, what is new in PowerShell 3.0?	1
Installation	2
Step 1 – what do I need?	2
Step 2 – downloading and installing Windows Management Framework	2
Step 3 – verifying that you have PowerShell v3 installed	4
And that's it	4
Quick start – configuring the default security policy in PowerShell	5
Top 7 features you need to know about	7
Using PowerShell for file and folder management in Windows Server Environment	7
Learning how to use PowerShell Web Access to manage your Windows Server Environment anywhere, anytime, and on any device	16
Step 1 — installing Windows PowerShell Web Access	17
Step 2 – configuring Windows PowerShell Web Access	18
Learning how to secure and sign the scripts you write using script signing	22
Learning how to manage the Active Directory environment	24
Resetting a user password	24
Disabling and Enabling a user account	25
Unlocking a user account	26
Deleting a user account	26
Working with groups	27
Adding members to a group	28
Enumerating the members of a group	28
Finding obsolete computer accounts	29
Disabling a computer account	29
Learning about the features included in the Microsoft.PowerShell. Security module	30
Learning how to use PowerShell to administer the PKI environment	31

Learning how to use the BPA module to analyze the security
integrity of a system as per Microsoft standards 34
People and places you should get to know **36**
Official sites 36
Articles and tutorials 36
Blogs 36
Twitter 37
About Packt Publishing 39
Writing for Packt 39

Instant Windows PowerShell

Windows PowerShell has been especially created to provide you with all the information that you need to get while setting up and running your Windows Server environment with PowerShell. In this book, you will learn the basics of PowerShell 3.0, get started with discovering various features in PowerShell, and discover some tips and tricks on how you can automate your Windows server environment with PowerShell.

This book holds the accompanying sections:

So, what's PowerShell? helps in finding out what PowerShell is, what you can do with it, various new features in it, and why it's so great.

Installation will help you learn how you can download and install PowerShell 3.0 with minimum fuss, and then set it up so that you can use it as soon as possible.

Quick start – configuring default security policy in PowerShell will give you an insight on the built-in default script security features in PowerShell 3.0.

Top 7 features you need to know about will teach you how to use the top seven features that can be implemented using various PowerShell modules and cmdlets.

People and places you should get to know provides you with many useful links to the project page and forums as well as a number of helpful articles, tutorials, blogs, and Twitter feeds of PowerShell super contributors.

So, what is new in PowerShell 3.0?

Windows PowerShell 3.0 includes various new features that enhance its ease of use and allow you to manage and administer your Windows-based environment.

Windows PowerShell 3.0 is compatible with the cmdlets, modules, snap-ins, scripts, functions, and profiles that are intended for Windows PowerShell 2.0.

Here is a list of some of the important new features present in PowerShell 3.0:

+ **Windows PowerShell Workflow**: Workflows are sequences of tasks, which can be repeated and also run parallel with other workflows. Workflows can be resumed after an interruption, such as a network outage, a Windows restart, or a power failure.

+ **Windows PowerShell Web Access**: This is a Windows Server 2012 feature that lets clients run Windows PowerShell scripts in an online web-based console.

+ **New Windows PowerShell ISE features**: For Windows PowerShell, Windows PowerShell **Integrated Scripting Environment** (**ISE**) has numerous new features, which include IntelliSense, Show-Command window, a unified console pane, and so on.

+ **Disconnected sessions**: In Windows PowerShell, persistent sessions (PSSessions) that you make by utilizing the `New-PSSession` cmdlet are safeguarded on the remote computer.

+ **Robust session connectivity**: Windows PowerShell 3.0 discovers an abrupt disconnection between the client and server, and attempts to restore connectivity and resume execution immediately. Assuming that the client-server association can't be restored in the dispensed time, the client is advised and the session is disengaged.

+ **Updatable help system**: You can now download the help documents for the cmdlets in your modules, and always have the latest up-to-date help. The `Update-Help` cmdlet recognizes the most current help files, downloads them from the Internet, unpacks them, accepts them, and installs them in the appropriate directory of the PowerShell module.

+ **CIM integration**: Windows PowerShell includes CIM cmdlets for standards-based management.

+ **Scheduled jobs and task scheduler integration**: You can now plan and schedule Windows PowerShell background jobs, and supervise them in Windows PowerShell and Windows Task Scheduler. Windows PowerShell-scheduled jobs are a combination of Windows PowerShell background jobs and task scheduler tasks.

+ **Module auto-loading**: You no longer need to import a module to use its cmdlets. In Windows PowerShell, you can just use any cmdlet and it would autoimport the module.

Installation

In the following steps, you will learn how to install and configure Windows PowerShell 3.0 and get it set up on your system.

Note that Windows PowerShell 3.0 comes preinstalled in Windows 8 and Windows Server 2012.

Step 1 – what do I need?

Before you install PowerShell 3.0, you will need to check that you have all the required elements, as follows:

+ A computer or server with a Windows 7 SP1 / 2008 SP2 / 2008R2 SP1 operating system
+ Access to the Internet
+ To use the latest version of PowerShell ISE, you would need to download, install, and configure Microsoft .NET Framework 4.0 Full from `http://go.microsoft.com/fwlink/?LinkID=212547`

Additionally, the following requirements apply:

+ To install the latest version of Windows PowerShell ISE for Windows PowerShell 3.0 on workstations running Windows Server 2008 R2 with Service Pack 1, before installing Windows Management Framework 3.0 RC, use Server Manager to add the Windows PowerShell ISE feature to Windows PowerShell.
+ Install the latest Windows updates before installing WMF 3.0 RC.

Step 2 – downloading and installing Windows Management Framework

Download and install the package based on your operating system version and architecture type, as shown in the following list:

+ For Windows 7 Service Pack 1, download and install the following packages:
    ◦ For 64-bit versions: `Windows6.1-KB2506143-x64.msu`
    ◦ For 32-bit versions: `Windows6.1-KB2506143-x86.msu`
+ For Windows Server 2008 R2 SP1, download and install the following package:
    ◦ For 64-bit versions: `Windows6.1-KB2506143-x64.msu`

♦ For Windows Server 2008 Service Pack 2, download and install the following packages:

　　° For 64-bit versions: `Windows6.0-KB2506146-x64.msu`

　　° For 32-bit versions: `Windows6.0-KB2506146-x86.msu`

Now to get these packages, you need to head over to the Microsoft Download Center at `http://www.microsoft.com/en-us/download/default.aspx` in your web browser and search for `Windows Management Framework 3.0-RC`, as shown in the following screenshot:

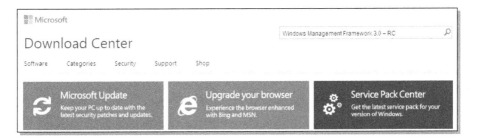

Next, click on the downloading icon for **Windows Management Framework 3.0 - RC** and initiate downloading of the Windows Management Framework 3.0 release notes document:

Close all instances of PowerShell hosts. Also, uninstall any previous builds of WMF 3.0, if installed.

Download and install the package applicable to your operating system version.

Step 3 – verifying that you have PowerShell v3 installed

Open a PowerShell window and type in the following:

PS C:\Windows\system32> $PSVersionTable

You will see that PSVersion (PowerShell version) now shows 3.0:

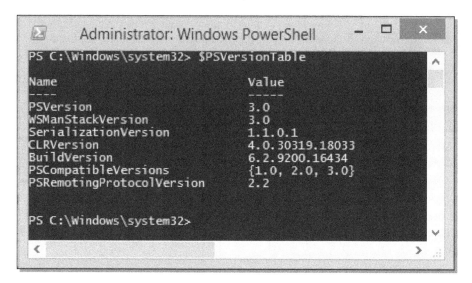

And that's it

It's really that easy. You just need to install and configure Windows Management Framework 3.0 to get going with Windows PowerShell V3.

It's still possible to get back to PowerShell V2 if needed.

The parameter to launch the PowerShell executable is
PS C:\Windows\system32> powershell.exe -version 2.

Quick start – configuring the default security policy in PowerShell

This section will give you an insight on the default script execution policy inbuilt in PowerShell 3.0. The execution policy determines if the PowerShell scripts' execution is disabled or enabled on the server. By default, the PowerShell script execution policy is set to **Restricted** in order to avoid any malicious code from running on your server; that means that scripts—including those you write yourself—won't run. You can verify the settings for your execution policy by typing the following in the PowerShell command prompt:

```
PS C:\> Get-ExecutionPolicy
```

You should now see the following screenshot:

If you want PowerShell to run any scripts that you write yourself or scripts downloaded from the Internet that have been signed by a trusted publisher, set your execution policy to **RemoteSigned**.

You can change the settings for your execution policy to **RemoteSigned** by typing the following in the PowerShell command prompt:

```
PS C:\> Set-ExecutionPolicy RemoteSigned
```

You should now see the following screenshot:

Alternatively, you can set the execution policy to **All Signed / Unrestricted**. Setting the execution policy to **Unrestricted** is insecure and not recommended in production environments.

The `Set-ExecutionPolicy` cmdlet changes the user preference for the Windows PowerShell execution policy by setting it in the registry `HKLM\SOFTWARE\Microsoft\PowerShell\1\` `ShellIds\Microsoft.PowerShell\ExecutionPolicy`.

On a 64-bit OS, you need to run `Set-ExecutionPolicy` for 32-bit and 64-bit PSH separately. You can change the `ExecutionPolicy` setting just once by specifying it in parameter when launching PowerShell:

```
PS C:\> powershell.exe -ExecutionPolicy Unrestricted
```

In that case, the execution policy is set in the variable `$env:PSExecutionPolicyPreference`.

For a more detailed help on script signing, you can type in the following command in your PowerShell console:

```
PS C:\> Get-Help about_Signing
```

You should now see the following screenshot:

Top 7 features you need to know about

Here you will learn various new features, which could be implemented using various PowerShell modules and cmdlets (command lets) to automate your Windows environment.

Using PowerShell for file and folder management in Windows Server Environment

In this section, I will illustrate some PowerShell cmdlets, which you can use for file and folder management using PowerShell:

✦ **Copy-Item**: The Copy-Item cmdlet copies an item from one location to another in a namespace. Copy-Item does not delete the items being copied. When the cmdlet is used with filesystems, it can be used to copy files and directories, and when used with Windows Registry, it can be used to copy registry keys and entries.

The following command will copy the file cmdout.log.txt to the C:\Presentation directory. The command does not delete the original file.

```
PS C:\> copy-item C:\vins\Logfiles\cmdout.log.txt -destination C:\
Presentation
```

The following command copies the entire content of the Log directory into the Backup directory. If the source directory contains files in subdirectories, those subdirectories will be copied with their file trees intact. The Container parameter is set to true by default. This preserves the directory structure.

```
PS C:\> copy-item C:\Log -destination C:\Backup -recurse
```

The default alias for the Copy-Item cmdlet is copy; you can use the cmdlet alias as follows:

```
PS C:\> copy C:\Log -destination C:\Backup -recurse
```

✦ **Get-Item**: The Get-Item cmdlet gets the item at the specified location. It does not get the contents of the item at the location unless you use a wildcard character (*) to request all the contents of the item. In the filesystem, the Get-Item cmdlet gets files and folders:

```
PS C:\> Get-Item
```

This command gets the current directory. The dot character (.) represents the item at the current location (not its contents):

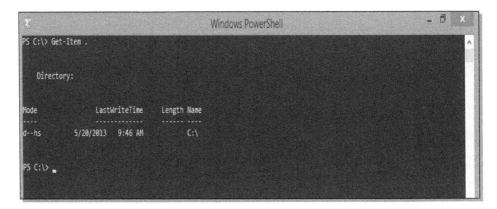

The following command gets the current directory of C : \:

```
PS C:\> Get-Item *
```

The object that is retrieved represents only the directory, not its contents:

```
PS C:\> Get-Item *

    Directory: C:\

Mode                LastWriteTime     Length Name
----                -------------     ------ ----
d----         12/7/2012  10:22 AM            drivers
d----          4/5/2013   3:55 PM            ExchangeSetupLogs
d----         1/29/2013   1:09 PM            hi
d----         2/15/2013   2:14 PM            HVRemote
d----        12/11/2012   1:13 PM            inetpub
d----         12/2/2012   9:15 AM            Intel
d----         12/1/2012   9:40 PM            JTD
d----         12/1/2012   8:56 PM            MININT
d----         4/29/2013   3:02 PM            OCPM Blog
d----         7/26/2012   1:03 PM            PerfLogs
d-r--         2/15/2013   3:34 PM            Program Files
d-r--         5/14/2013  11:27 AM            Program Files (x86)
d----         1/16/2013  10:33 AM            Quarantine
d----         12/4/2012   9:06 AM            temp
d-r--          5/7/2013   9:18 PM            Users
d----         3/20/2013   1:00 PM            Vinith
d----          5/9/2013   2:41 PM            vinithtest
d----         5/20/2013   9:45 AM            Windows
d----        12/11/2012   1:13 PM            Windows.old
-a---         1/16/2013   5:04 PM          0 Counter.csv
-a---         5/23/2012   8:28 PM  255739392 Setup_CamtasiaStudio8_x86_ENU.msi

PS C:\>
```

The following command gets the items in C : \:

```
PS C:\> Get-Item C:\
```

The wildcard character (*) represents all the items in the container, not just the container. You should see the following screenshot now:

The following command gets the `LastAccessTime` property of the `C:\Windows` directory. `LastAccessTime`, as shown in the following command, is just one property of the file system object:

```
PS C:\> (Get-Item C:\Windows).LastAccessTime
```

You should now see the following screenshot:

```
Windows PowerShell
PS C:\> (Get-Item C:\Windows).LastAccessTime
Monday, May 20, 2013 9:45:51 AM
PS C:\>
```

The following command gets items in the Windows directory with names that include a dot (.), but do not begin with w*. This command works only when the path includes a wildcard character (*) to specify the contents of the item:

```
PS C:\> Get-Item C:\Windows\*.* -Exclude w*
```

You should now get the following screenshot:

```
Windows PowerShell
PS C:\> Get-Item C:\Windows\*.* -Exclude w*

    Directory: C:\Windows

Mode                LastWriteTime     Length Name
----                -------------     ------ ----
d----        5/20/2013  10:12 AM             Microsoft.NET
-a---        7/31/2012  12:25 AM          0 authtest.txt
-a---        7/26/2012   8:38 AM      75264 bfsvc.exe
-a--s        5/20/2013   9:38 AM      67584 bootstat.dat
-a---       12/30/2012   2:42 PM        257 csplayer.ini
-a---       12/11/2012  12:07 AM       6510 comsetup.log
-a---        1/17/2013   2:42 PM       1998 diagerr.xml
-a---        1/17/2013   2:42 PM       2207 diagwrn.xml
-a---       11/17/2005   1:16 PM     414632 difxapi.dll
-a---         3/5/2013   3:26 PM      37896 DPINST.LOG
-a---       12/11/2012  12:00 AM       3952 DtcInstall.log
-a---        7/26/2012   1:45 AM      31881 Enterprise.xml
-a---        7/26/2012  10:19 AM    2300640 explorer.exe
-a---        7/26/2012   8:38 AM     883712 HelpPane.exe
-a---        7/26/2012   8:38 AM      17400 hh.exe
-a---       12/10/2012  11:58 PM      21658 iis.log
-a---         1/9/2013   8:53 AM  496784843 MEMORY.DMP
-a---        7/26/2012   2:02 AM      43131 mib.bin
-a---        6/11/2009   2:06 AM       1405 msdfmap.ini
-a---        7/26/2012   8:38 AM     243712 notepad.exe
-a---        1/10/2013  12:07 PM        162 ODBC.INI
-a---         5/7/2013   8:56 PM      12352 PERD.log
-a---        5/16/2013   7:02 PM    2693728 PWBBTHLV.EXE
-a---        7/26/2012   8:38 AM     159232 regedit.exe
-a---        5/20/2013   9:38 AM    1003220 setupact.log
-a---        1/17/2013   2:42 PM          0 setuperr.log
-a---        12/1/2012   7:48 PM         36 sModel.txt
-a---        5/20/2013   9:47 AM        535 SMSCFG.ini
-a---        12/1/2012   8:15 PM         51 smslt.ini
-a---        7/26/2012   8:38 AM     126464 splwow64.exe
-a---        7/26/2012   1:45 AM      31537 Starter.xml
-a---        7/26/2012  10:56 AM        219 system.ini
-a---       12/2/2012    9:17 AM       8063 TSSysprep.log
-a---        7/26/2012   8:50 AM      50176 twain_32.dll
-a---        7/28/2012  12:57 PM       1585 vmgcoinstall.log
PS C:\>
```

The default alias for the Get-Item cmdlet is gi; you can use the cmdlet alias as follows:

```
PS C:\> gi C:\Windows\*.* -Exclude w*
```

✦ **Get-ItemProperty**: The Get-ItemProperty cmdlet gets the properties of the specified items. For example, you can use Get-ItemProperty to get the value of the LastAccessTime property of a file or folder object. You can also use Get-ItemProperty to view registry entries and their values:

```
PS C:\> Get-ItemProperty C:\Windows
```

The previous command gets information about the C:\Windows directory:

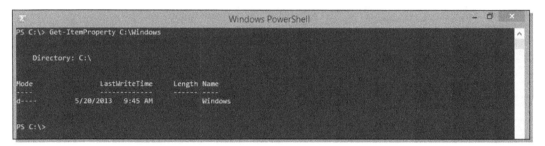

The following command gets the properties of the C:\Windows\bfsvc.exe file:

```
PS C:\> Get-ItemProperty C:\Windows\bfsvc.exe | Format-List
```

The result is piped to the Format-List cmdlet to display the output as a list:

```
PS C:\> Get-ItemProperty C:\Windows\bfsvc.exe | Format-List


    Directory: C:\Windows


Name           : bfsvc.exe
Length         : 75264
CreationTime   : 7/26/2012 7:29:23 AM
LastWriteTime  : 7/26/2012 8:38:18 AM
LastAccessTime : 7/26/2012 7:29:23 AM
VersionInfo    : File:             C:\Windows\bfsvc.exe
                 InternalName:     bfsvc.exe
                 OriginalFilename: bfsvc.exe.mui
                 FileVersion:      6.2.9200.16384 (win8_rtm.120725-1247)
                 FileDescription:  Boot File Servicing Utility
                 Product:          Microsoft® Windows® Operating System
                 ProductVersion:   6.2.9200.16384
                 Debug:            False
                 Patched:          False
                 PreRelease:       False
                 PrivateBuild:     False
                 SpecialBuild:     False
                 Language:         English (United States)



PS C:\>
```

The default alias for the `Get-Item` cmdlet is `gi`; you can use the cmdlet alias as follows:

```
PS C:\> gp C:\Windows\bfsvc.exe | Format-List
```

✦ **Invoke-Item**: The `Invoke-Item` cmdlet performs the default action on the specified item. For example, it runs an executable file or opens a document file in the application associated with the document file type. The default action depends on the type of item and is determined by the Windows PowerShell provider that provides access to the data.

The following command opens the file alias `counter.csv` in Microsoft Excel:

```
PS C :\> invoke-item C:\Counter.csv
```

In this case, opening in Excel is the default action for `.csv` files. You should now see the following screenshot:

The following command opens all of the Microsoft Office Excel spreadsheets in the `C:\Documents and Settings\sample\My Documents` folder:

```
PS C:\> invoke-item "C:\Documents and Settings\sample\My
Documents\*.xls"
```

Each spreadsheet is opened in a new instance of Excel. In this case, opening in Excel is the default action for the `.xls` files. You should now see the following screenshot:

The default alias for the `Invoke-Item` cmdlet is `ii`; you can use the cmdlet alias as follows:

```
PS C:\> ii C:\Counter.csv | Format-List
```

✦ **Move-Item**: The `Move-Item` cmdlet moves an item, including its properties, contents, and child items, from one location to another. The locations must be supported by the same provider. For example, it can move a file or subdirectory from one directory to another, or move a registry subkey from one key to another. When you move an item, it is added to the new location and deleted from its original location.

```
PS C:\> move-item -path C:\test.txt -destination E:\Temp\tst.txt
```

The previous command moves the `Test.txt` file from the `C:\` drive to the `E:\Temp` directory and renames it from `test.txt` to `tst.txt`, as shown in the following screenshot:

The following command moves all of the text files (`*.txt`) in the current directory (represented by a dot (`.`)) to the `C:\Logs` directory:

```
PS C:\> move-item -path .\*.txt -destination C:\Logs
```

You should now see the following screenshot:

The following command moves all of the text files from the current directory and all subdirectories, recursively, to the `C:\TextFiles` directory:

```
PS C:\> Get-ChildItem -Path .\*.txt -Recurse | Move-Item
-Destination C:\TextFiles
```

You should now see the following screenshot:

The default alias for the `Move-Item` cmdlet is `move`, `mi`, or `mv`; you can use the cmdlet alias as follows:

```
PS C:\> move .\*.txt -destination C:\Logs
```

```
PS C:\> mi .\*.txt -destination C:\Logs
```

```
PS C:\> mv .\*.txt -destination C:\Logs
```

✦ **New-Item**: The `New-Item` cmdlet creates a new item and sets its value. The types of items that can be created depend upon the location of the item. For example, in the filesystem, `New-Item` is used to create files and folders. In the registry, `New-Item` creates registry keys and entries.

```
PS C:\> new-item -path c:\vinith testfile12.txt -itemtype "file"
-value "This is a text string."
```

The previous command creates a text file named `testfile1.txt` in the `c:\vinith` directory. The dot (`.`) in the value of the `Path` parameter indicates the current directory. The quoted text that follows the `Value` parameter is added to the file as content:

The following command creates a directory named `Logfiles` in the `C:\` directory:

```
PS C:\> new-item -path c:\ -name logfiles -itemtype directory
```

The `ItemType` parameter specifies that the new item is a directory, not a file or some other filesystem object, as shown in the following screenshot:

```
Windows PowerShell                                    _ □ ×
PS C:\> new-item -path c:\ -name logfiles -itemtype directory


    Directory: C:\


Mode                LastWriteTime     Length Name
----                -------------     ------ ----
d----         5/20/2013  11:01 AM            logfiles


PS C:\> _
```

The following command uses the `New-Item` cmdlet to create files in two different directories:

```
PS C:\> new-item -itemtype file -path "c:\ps-test\test12.txt",
"c:\ps-test\Logs\test12.log"
```

Because the `Path` parameter takes multiple strings, you can use it to create multiple items. You can now see the following screenshot:

The default alias for the `New-Item` cmdlet is `ni`. You can use the cmdlet alias as follows:

```
PS C:\> ni -path c:\ -name logfiles -itemtype directory
```

✦ **Remove-Item**: The `Remove-Item` cmdlet deletes one or more items. Because it is supported by many providers, it can delete many different types of items, including files, directories, registry keys, variables, aliases, and functions. In filesystem drives, the `Remove-Item` cmdlet deletes files and folders.

```
C:\PS>Remove-Item C:\Test\*.*
```

This command deletes all the files with names that include a dot (.) from the `C:\Test` directory. Because the command specifies a dot, the command does not delete directories or files with no file name extension. You should now see the following screenshot:

The following command deletes a file that is both hidden and read-only:

```
C:\PS>Remove-Item -Path C:\Test\Invisible-ROnly-file.txt -Force
```

It uses the `Path` parameter to specify the file. It uses the `Force` parameter to give permission to delete it. Without `Force`, you cannot delete read-only or hidden files.

The default alias for the `Remove-Item` cmdlet is `del`, `erase`, `rd`, `ri`, `rm`, and `rmdir`. You can use the cmdlet alias as follows:

```
C:\PS> del -Path C:\Test\Invisible-ROnly-file.txt -Force

C:\PS> erase -Path C:\Test\Invisible-ROnly-file.txt -Force


C:\PS> rd -Path C:\Test\Invisible-ROnly-file.txt -Force


C:\PS> ri -Path C:\Test\Invisible-ROnly-file.txt -Force


C:\PS> rm -Path C:\Test\Invisible-ROnly-file.txt -Force
```

✦ **Get-Acl**: The `Get-Acl` cmdlet gets objects that represent the security descriptor of a file or resource. The security descriptor contains the **access control lists** (**ACLs**) of the resource in an array. The ACL specifies the permissions that users and user groups have to access the resource.

The following command gets the security descriptor of the `C:\Windows` directory:

```
PS C:\> Get-Acl C:\Windows
```

You should now see the following screenshot:

✦ **Set-Acl**: The `Set-Acl` cmdlet changes the security descriptor of a specified item, such as a file or a registry key, to match the values in a security descriptor that you supply. To use `Set-Acl`, use the `Path` parameter to identify the item whose security descriptor you want to change. Then, use the `AclObject` parameters to supply a security descriptor that has the values you want to apply.

The following commands copy the values from the security descriptor of the `123.csv` file to the security descriptor of the `123.html` file:

```
PS C:\> $ACL = Get-Acl C:\vinith\123.csv
PS C:\> Set-Acl -Path  C:\vinith\123.html -AclObject $ACL
```

When the execution of the commands is complete, the security descriptors of the `123.csv` and `123.html` files are identical. The following screenshot shows the usage of the commands:

The following command is almost the same as the command in the previous example, except that it uses a pipeline operator to send the security descriptor from a `Get-Acl` command to a `Set-Acl` command:

```
PS C:\> Get-Acl C:\vinith\123.csv | Set-Acl -Path C:\vinith\123.html
```

The following commands apply the security descriptors in the `123.csv` file to all text files in the `C:\Temp` directory and all of its subdirectories:

```
PS C:\> $NewAcl = Get-Acl C:\vinith\123.csv
```

```
PS C:\> Get-ChildItem c:\temp -Recurse -Include *.txt -Force | Set-Acl -AclObject $NewAcl
```

You should now see the following screenshot:

![Administrator: Windows PowerShell screenshot showing the commands executed]

Learning how to use PowerShell Web Access to manage your Windows Server Environment anywhere, anytime, and on any device

PowerShell Web Access, a web-based Windows PowerShell console, and Windows PowerShell commands and scripts can be run from a Windows PowerShell console in a web browser; with no Windows PowerShell, remote management software, or browser plug-in installation becomes necessary on the client device.

All that is required to run the web-based Windows PowerShell console is a properly configured Windows PowerShell Web Access gateway, and a client device browser that supports JavaScript and accepts cookies.

Examples of client devices include laptops, tablet computers, web kiosks, computers that are not running a Windows-based operating system, and cell phone browsers. IT pros can perform critical management tasks on remote Windows-based servers from devices that have access to an Internet connection and a web browser.

Users can access a Windows PowerShell console by using a web browser. When users open the secured Windows PowerShell Web Access website, they can run a web-based Windows PowerShell console after successful authentication, as shown in the following screenshot:

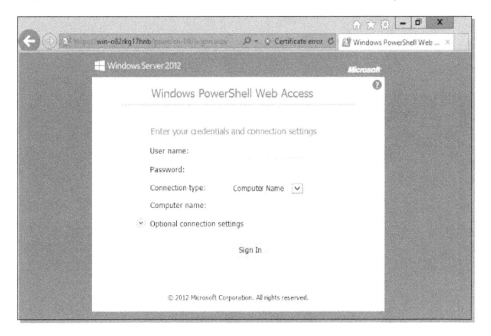

Here are the steps that I followed to test **PSWA** (**PowerShell Web Access**).

Step 1 — installing Windows PowerShell Web Access

Run the following command:

```
PS C:\Users\Administrator> Install-WindowsFeature
WindowsPowerShellWebAccess
```

You should now see the following screen:

```
PS C:\Users\Administrator> Install-WindowsFeature WindowsPowerShellWebAccess

Success Restart Needed Exit Code     Feature Result
------- -------------- ---------     --------------
True    Yes            SuccessRest... {Windows PowerShell Web Access}
WARNING: You must restart this server to finish the installation process.
WARNING: For more information about how to finish installing and configuring Windows PowerShell Web Access, see
http://go.microsoft.com/fwlink/?LinkID=221050.

PS C:\Users\Administrator>
```

Once we install PowerShell Web Access, we need to start to configuring it.

Step 2 – configuring Windows PowerShell Web Access

We will configure Windows PowerShell Web Access by installing the web application and configuring a predefined gateway rule. Now, create just a test certificate and an SSL binding using that certificate for a test environment:

```
PS C:\Users\Administrator> Install-PswaWebApplication -useTestCertificate
```

After this, you should see the following screenshot:

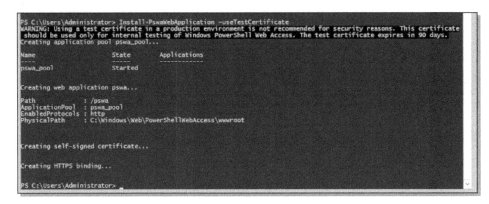

Now, set the authorization rule on which all can have rights for PowerShell Web Access; for my test environment, I set it to *, which means all have access:

```
PS C:\Users\Administrator> Add-PswaAuthorizationRule -ComputerName *
-UserName * -ConfigurationName *
```

This step gives the following output:

Now if you run a Get-PswaAuthorizationRule command, you can see the list of users having access to PSWA:

```
PS C:\Users\Administrator> Get-PswaAuthorizationRule
```

The following screenshot shows the output:

Now that PowerShell Web Access is set up, we can access the PSWA page via a web browser. You get an error message, **Error! Hyperlink reference not valid**. You should see the following options on the screen:

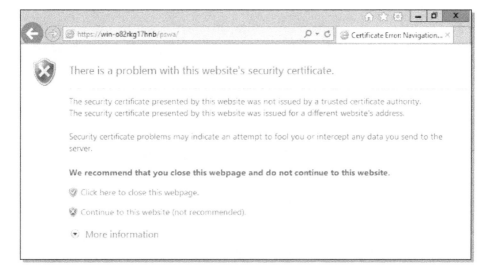

You will receive this error because you are using a test certificate that cannot be validated; click on **Continue to this website (not recommended)**.

You will now reach the following page:

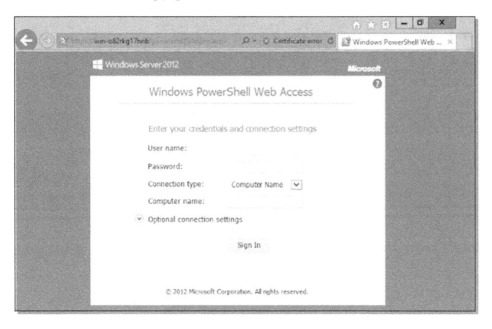

Now enter the username and password to connect to a remote computer, which also accepts IP addresses (specified in computer name block), and voila! You are now logged into the remote console of the server:

Run a hostname command, `$psversiontable`, and also query `wmi` for the operating system installed on your remote system, and it indeed shows that you were logged into the correct host and it also had PowerShell v2 installed:

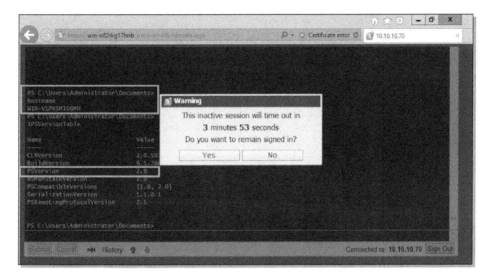

I also wanted to share one more screen along with this example for **inactive session timeout** which autologged off my session when I was inactive for a certain period of time:

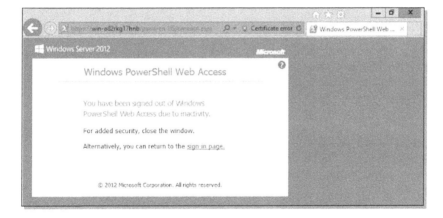

Now let's see a real-world example of PowerShell Web Access. Here's the console when I accessed it from my Android tablet.

So, we can see that with PSWA you can get a fully fledged PowerShell environment on my handheld device:

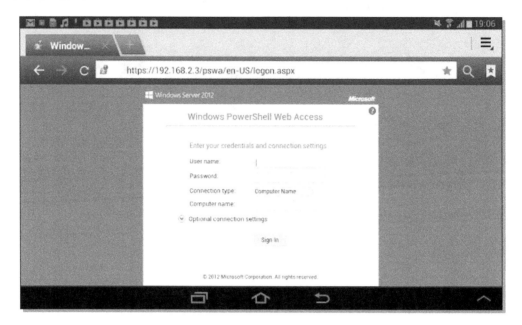

Learning how to secure and sign the scripts you write using script signing

There are basically two PowerShell cmdlets, which you can use to sign your scripts. Signing your scripts is like imprinting them with a rubber stamp so that the scripts would maintain an identity of who created them. Usually, I in a production environment, the execution policy is set to `allsigned`, which means that only signed scripts are allowed to run. The `(Get/Set)-Authenticode Signature` cmdlet can be used to work with script signing.

✦ **Get-AuthenticodeSignature**: The `Get-AuthenticodeSignature` cmdlet gets information about the Authenticode signature in a file. If the file is not signed, the information is retrieved, but the fields are blank.

```
PS C:\> Get-AuthenticodeSignature C:\Vinith\Export-
NaEfficiencyXls.ps1
```

After running the previous command, you should see the following screen:

This command gets information about the Authenticode signature in the `Export-NaEfficiencyXls.ps1` file. It uses the `FilePath` parameter to specify the file.

✦ **Set-AuthenticodeSignature**: The `Set-AuthenticodeSignature` cmdlet adds an Authenticode signature to any file that supports **Subject Interface Package** (**SIP**). In a Windows PowerShell script file, the signature takes the form of a block of text that indicates the end of the instructions that are executed in the script. If there is a signature in the file when this cmdlet runs, that signature is removed.

Here are some examples on how you can use these cmdlets:

○ The following command retrieves a code-signing certificate from the Windows PowerShell certificate provider and uses it to sign a Windows PowerShell script:

```
PS C:\> $cert=Get-ChildItem -Path cert:\CurrentUser\my
-CodeSigningCert
```

○ The following commands use the `Get-PfxCertificate` cmdlet to find a code-signing certificate. Then, they use it to sign a Windows PowerShell script:

```
PS C:\> $cert = Get-PfxCertificate C:\Test\Mysign.pfx

PS C:\>Set-AuthenticodeSignature -Filepath Export-NaEfficiencyXls.
ps1 -Cert $cert
```

1. The first command uses the `Get-PfxCertificate` cmdlet to find the `C:\Test\MySign.pfx` certificate and store it in the `$cert` variable.

2. The second command uses `Set-AuthenticodeSignature` to sign the script. The `FilePath` parameter of `Set-AuthenticodeSignature` specifies the path to the script file being signed, and the `Cert` parameter passes the `$cert` variable containing the certificate to `Set-AuthenticodeSignature`.

3. If the certificate file is password protected, Windows PowerShell prompts you for the password.

Learning how to manage the Active Directory environment

You can carry out most of your routine Active Directory tasks using PowerShell and automate them via scripts; most of the activities which you can perform to secure your AD environment can be done using PowerShell.

Open a PowerShell session and import the Active Directory module:

```
PS C:\> Import-Module ActiveDirectory
```

To see a list of cmdlets which are a part of the Active Directory module, type in the following command:

```
PS C:\> get-command -module ActiveDirectory
```

You should now get the following screenshot:

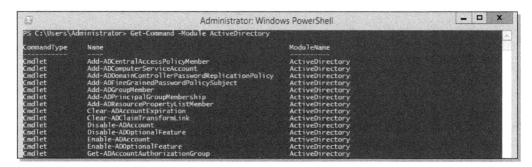

Now let's work on some basic Active Directory security tasks, which you can perform using PowerShell.

Resetting a user password

Let's start with a frequently used typical IT task, resetting a user's password. We can easily accomplish this by using the Set-ADAccountPassword cmdlet. The password must be specified as a secure string:

```
PS C:\> $new = Read-Host "Enter the new password" -AsSecureString
PS C:\> Set-ADAccountPassword user1 -NewPassword $new
```

The output screen should look as follows:

PS C:\> Set-ADAccountPassword user1 –NewPassword (ConvertTo-SecureString -AsPlainText –String "P@ssw3@%%@%%@" -force)

To change user's password at his or her next logon, we can use `Set-ADUser`:

```
PS C:\> Set-ADUser user1 -ChangePasswordAtLogon $True
```

The output screen should look as follows:

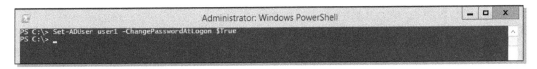

The command doesn't write to the pipeline or console unless you use `True`.

Disabling and Enabling a user account

We can use a `-whatif` parameter to see the changes prior to committing them:

```
PS C:\> Disable-ADAccount user1 -whatif
```

```
PS C:\> Disable-ADAccount user1
```

Now to enable this account, we can use `Enable-ADAccount`:

```
PS C:\> Enable-ADAccount user1
```

You should now see the following screenshot:

These cmdlets can be used in a pipelined expression to enable or disable as many accounts as you need. For example, the following command disables all user accounts in the sales department:

```
PS C:\> get-aduser -filter "department -eq 'contractor'" | disable-
adaccount
```

Unlocking a user account

Rather than digging through the GUI to find an account, you can unlock it by using the following simple command:

```
PS C:\> Unlock-ADAccount Vins
```

You should see the output screen as follows:

This cmdlet also supports the -Whatif and -Confirm parameters.

Deleting a user account

You can use the following command to delete a user account:

```
PS C:\> Remove-ADUser Vins -whatif
```

You should now see the following output screen:

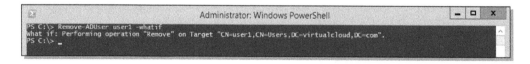

We can also use PowerShell pipeline to remove a bunch of users and delete them with one simple command:

```
PS C:\> get-aduser -filter "enabled -eq 'false'"
```

```
-property WhenChanged -SearchBase "OU=Employees,
DC=virtualcloud,DC=Local" | where {$_.WhenChanged
-le (Get-Date).AddDays(-360)} | Remove-ADuser -whatif
```

This one-line command would find and delete all disabled accounts in the employees'
organizational unit (**OU**) that haven't been changed in at least 360 days.

Working with groups

The following code will find all groups in the domain which are empty or do not have any users in
them, including built-in groups:

```
PS C:\> get-adgroup -filter * | where {-Not($_ | get-adgroupmember)} |
Select Name
```

You should get the output as shown in the following screenshot:

Adding members to a group

Let's add user1 to the Hyper-V Administrators group:

```
PS C:\> add-adgroupmember " Hyper-V Administrators" -Members user1
```

You should now see the output as shown in the following screenshot:

Enumerating the members of a group

You might want to see who belongs to a given group. For this, you can use the following command:

```
PS C:\> Get-ADGroupMember " Hyper-V Administrators"
```

You should see the output as shown in the following screenshot:

The cmdlet writes an AD object for each member to the pipeline.

To get a list of all user accounts in nested user groups, all you need to do is use the -Recursive parameter:

```
PS C:\> Get-ADGroupMember " Hyper-V Administrators" -Recursive | Select
DistinguishedName
```

Finding obsolete computer accounts

Assuming that a computer hasn't changed its password with the domain in a particular period of time, use the following command to filter and find the obsolete computer accounts:

```
PS C:\> get-adcomputer -filter "Passwordlastset -lt '1/1/2013'"
-properties *| Select name,passwordlastset
```

You should see the filtered computer accounts, as shown in the following screenshot:

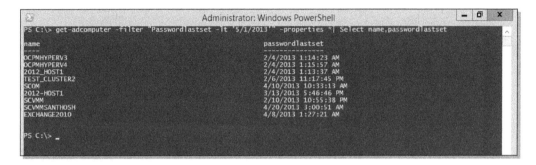

The filter works best with a hard-coded value, but this code will retrieve all computer accounts that haven't changed their password since May 1, 2013.

Disabling a computer account

You can specify which computer account to disable by using the account's `samAccountname` value:

```
PS C:\> get-adcomputer "scvmm1" | Disable-ADAccount
```

You should see the output as shown in the following screenshot:

For more information on the list of cmdlets which can be used for Active Directory administration, please refer to
`http://technet.microsoft.com/en-us/library/hh852274(v=wps.620).aspx`.

Learning about the features included in the Microsoft. PowerShell.Security module

In this section, I will provide you with some basic cmdlets, which are a part of the `Microsoft.PowerShell.Security` module:

+ **ConvertFrom-SecureString**: The `ConvertFrom-SecureString` cmdlet converts a secure string (`System.Security.SecureString`) into an encrypted standard string (`System.String`). Unlike a secure string, an encrypted standard string can be saved in a file for later use. The encrypted standard string can be converted back to its secure string format by using the `ConvertTo-SecureString` cmdlet.

   The following command reads a set of characters from a user and stores it as a secure string in the $securestring variable:

   ```
   PS C:\> $SecureString = Read-Host -AsSecureString
   ```

   The following command converts the secure string in the $SecureString variable to an encrypted standard string:

   ```
   PS C:\> $StandardString = ConvertFrom-SecureString  $SecureString
   ```

   The resulting encrypted standard string is stored in the $StandardString variable. You should see the output screen as follows:

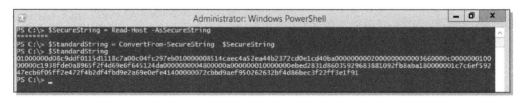

+ **ConvertTo-SecureString**: The `ConvertTo-SecureString` cmdlet converts encrypted standard strings into secure strings. It can additionally convert plain text to secure strings. The secure string can be converted back to an encrypted, standard string utilizing the `ConvertFrom-SecureString` cmdlet. This enables it to be stored in a file for later use.

   If the standard string being converted was encrypted with `ConvertFrom-SecureString` utilizing a specified key, that same key must be provided as the value of the `Key` or `SecureKey` parameter of the `ConvertTo-SecureString` cmdlet.

   The following command converts the plain text string P@ssW0rD! into a secure string and stores the result in the $secure_string_pwd variable:

   ```
   PS C:\> $secure_string_pwd = convertto-securestring "P@ssW0rD!"
   -asplaintext -force
   ```

To utilize the `AsPlainText` parameter, the `Force` parameter must additionally be included in the command. You should now see the output screen as follows:

Learning how to use PowerShell to administer the PKI environment

In order to get started with administrating PKI, we should first import the PKI module:

PS C:\> Import-Module PKI

In the following list I will show you some basic cmdlets, which you can use to administer the PKI environment:

+ **Export-Certificate**: The `Export-Certificate` cmdlet exports a certificate from a certificate store to a file. The private key is not included in the export if more than one certificate is being exported.

  Here is an example of the `Export-Certificate` cmdlet in action:

  PS C:\> $cert = (Get-ChildItem -Path Cert:\CurrentUser\My\ C33B8174F1487B2DE2778D7BB7441F89A6709D3B)

  Utilize the `Type` parameter to transmute the file format:

  PS C:\> Export-Certificate -Cert $cert -FilePath c:\certs\user.sst -Type SST

This example exports a certificate to the filesystem as a Microsoft serialized certificate store without its private key:

```
PS C:\> $cert = (Get-ChildItem -Path Cert:\CurrentUser\My\
C33B8174F1487B2DE2778D7BB7441F89A6709D3B)

PS C:\> Export-Certificate -Cert $cert -FilePath c:\certs\user.cer
```

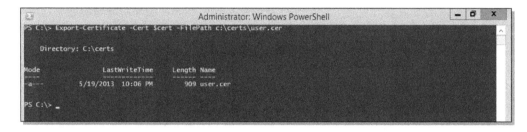

This example exports a certificate to the file system as a DER-encoded .cer file without its private key.

This following commands export all certificates under the CurrentUser\my store into a Microsoft serialized certificate store allcerts.sst:

```
PS C:\> $cert = (Get-ChildItem -Path cert:\CurrentUser\My\
EEDEF61D4FF6EDBAAD538BB08CCAADDC3EE28FF)


PS C:\> Get-ChildItem -Path cert:\CurrentUser\my | Export-
Certificate -FilePath c:\certs\allcerts.sst -Type SST
```

You should get the output as shown in the following screenshot:

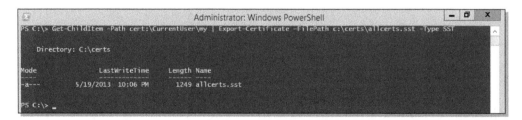

✦ **Get-Certificate** : The Get-Certificate cmdlet can be acclimated to submit a certificate request and install the resulting certificate, install a certificate from a pending certificate request, and enroll for ldap. If the request is issued, the returned certificate is installed in the store resolute by the CertStoreLocation parameter and returns the certificate in the EnrollmentResult structure with status Issued.

Delegation may be required when utilizing this cmdlet with Windows PowerShell remoting and transmuting utilizer configuration.

The following commands submit a certificate request for the SslWebServer template to the specific URL using the username and password credentials:

```
PS C:\> $up = Get-Credential
```

```
PS C:\> Get-Certificate -Template SslWebServer -DnsName www.
virtualcloud.com -Url `

https://www.virtualcloud.com/Policy/service.svc -Credential $up
-CertStoreLocation ` cert:\LocalMachine\My
```

You should see the output as shown in the following screenshot:

```
Administrator: Windows PowerShell                                    _ ☐ X
PS C:\> $up = Get-Credential
cmdlet Get-Credential at command pipeline position 1
Supply values for the following parameters:
Credential
PS C:\> Get-Certificate -Template SslWebServer -DnsName www.virtualcloud.com -Url `
>> https://www.virtualcloud.com/Policy/service.svc -Credential $up -CertStoreLocation ` cert:\LocalMachine\My
>>
PS C:\> _
```

In the previous example, the request will have two DNS names in it. This is for a certificate in the machine store. If the request is issued, the returned certificate is installed in the machine's MY store and the certificate in the EnrollmentResult structure is returned with the status Issued.

If the request is pending, it is installed in the machine's REQUEST store. The request in the EnrollmentResult structure is returned with the status Pending.

Learning how to use the BPA module to analyze the security integrity of a system as per Microsoft standards

The following list shows the cmdlets, which can be used to learn how to use the BPA module to analyze the security integrity of a system as per Microsoft requirements:

✦ **Get-BpaModel**: The Get-BpaModel cmdlet retrieves and displays the list of models that are supported by **Best Practices Analyzer (BPA)** and installed on the computer:

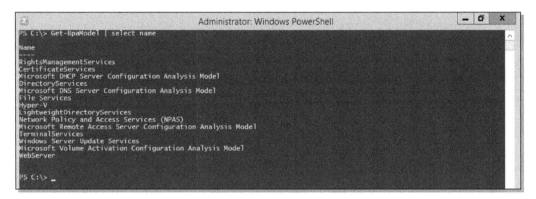

✦ **Get-BpaResult**: The Get-BpaResult cmdlet retrieves and displays the results of the latest BPA scan for a specific model that is installed on a computer. To use this cmdlet, add the ModelId parameter, and specify the model identifier (ID) for which to view the most recent BPA scan results.

The following is an example when im is extracting the results of the Hyper-V model ID:

```
PS C:\> Get-BpaResult -ModelId Microsoft/Windows/Hyper-V | select
title,compliance | fl *
```

You should see the output as shown in the following screenshot:

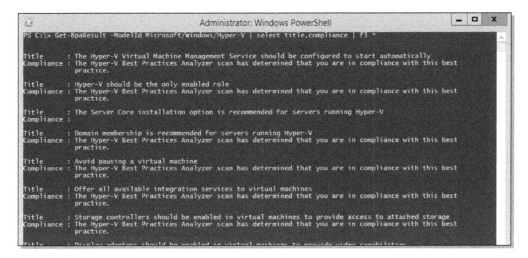

+ **Invoke-BpaModel**: The `Invoke-BpaModel` cmdlet starts a BPA scan for a specific model that is installed on a Windows-based computer. The model is specified either by using the `ModelId` parameter, or by piping the results of the `Get-BpaModel` cmdlet into this cmdlet:

```
PS C:\> Invoke-BpaModel -Id Microsoft/Windows/Hyper-V
```

You should see the output as shown in the following screenshot:

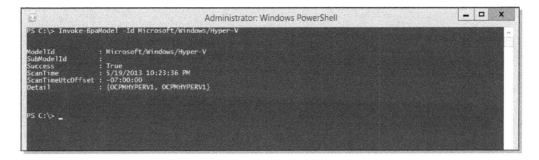

People and places you should get to know

PowerShell has great community support. This section provides you with many useful links to the project page and forums, as well as a number of helpful articles, tutorials, blogs, and the Twitter feeds of PowerShell's super contributors.

Official sites

✦ Homepage: `http://msdn.microsoft.com/en-us/library/windows/desktop/dd835506(v=vs.85).aspx`

✦ Manual and documentation: `http://technet.microsoft.com/library/bb978526.aspx`

✦ Wiki: `http://social.technet.microsoft.com/wiki/contents/articles/183.windows-powershell-survival-guide.aspx`

✦ Blog: `http://blogs.msdn.com/b/powershell/`

Articles and tutorials

✦ A video playlist from the "PowerShell Guru" *Don Jones* displaying all cool features of PowerShell is available at `http://www.youtube.com/user/powershelldon`. A must watch!

✦ Refer to the *PowerShell—Working With Regular Expressions (regex)* article at `http://social.technet.microsoft.com/wiki/contents/articles/4310.powershell-working-with-regular-expressions-regex.aspx`

✦ Refer to the *PowerShell—Advanced Function Parameter Attributes* article at `http://social.technet.microsoft.com/wiki/contents/articles/15994.powershell-advanced-function-parameter-attributes.aspx`

Blogs

✦ The blog by PowerShell MVP's *PowerShell* magazine at `http://www.powershellmagazine.com/`

✦ POWERSHELL PRO!: `http://www.powershellpro.com/powershell-tutorial-introduction/`

✦ PowerShell.com: `http://powershell.com/cs/`

✦ PowerShellbooks.com :`http://www.powershellbooks.com/`

✦ PowerShell.org: `http://powershell.org/wp/`

Twitter

- ✦ Follow *PowerShellMagazine* on Twitter at @PowerShellMag
- ✦ Follow *PowerScripting* on Twitter at @powerscripting
- ✦ Follow *ShayLevy* on Twitter at @ShayLevy
- ✦ Follow *Glenn Sizemore* on Twitter at @glnsize

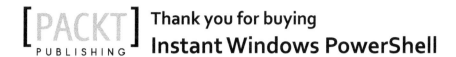

About Packt Publishing

Packt, pronounced 'packed', published its first book "*Mastering phpMyAdmin for Effective MySQL Management*" in April 2004 and subsequently continued to specialize in publishing highly focused books on specific technologies and solutions.

Our books and publications share the experiences of your fellow IT professionals in adapting and customizing today's systems, applications, and frameworks. Our solution based books give you the knowledge and power to customize the software and technologies you're using to get the job done. Packt books are more specific and less general than the IT books you have seen in the past. Our unique business model allows us to bring you more focused information, giving you more of what you need to know, and less of what you don't.

Packt is a modern, yet unique publishing company, which focuses on producing quality, cutting-edge books for communities of developers, administrators, and newbies alike. For more information, please visit our website: www.packtpub.com.

Writing for Packt

We welcome all inquiries from people who are interested in authoring. Book proposals should be sent to author@packtpub.com. If your book idea is still at an early stage and you would like to discuss it first before writing a formal book proposal, contact us; one of our commissioning editors will get in touch with you.

We're not just looking for published authors; if you have strong technical skills but no writing experience, our experienced editors can help you develop a writing career, or simply get some additional reward for your expertise.

Windows Server 2012
Automation with PowerShell
Cookbook

Over 110 recipes to automate Windows Server administrative
tasks using PowerShell

Ed Goad

Windows Server 2012 Automation with PowerShell Cookbook

ISBN: 978-1-84968-946-5   Paperback: 372 pages

Over 110 recipes to automate Windows Server
administrative tasks using PowerShell

1. Extend the capabilities of your Windows
   environment

2. Improve the process reliability by using well defined
   PowerShell scripts

3. Full of examples, scripts, and real-world best
   practices

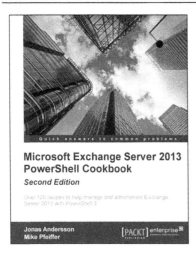

Microsoft Exchange Server 2013
PowerShell Cookbook
Second Edition

Jonas Andersson
Mike Pfeiffer

Microsoft Exchange Server 2013 PowerShell Cookbook: Second Edition

ISBN: 978-1-84968-942-7   Paperback:504 pages

Over 120 recipes to help manage and administrate
Exchange Server 2013 with PowerShell 3

1. Newly updated and improved for Exchange Server
   2013 and PowerShell 3

2. Learn how to write scripts and functions, schedule
   scripts to run automatically, and generate complex
   reports with PowerShell

3. Manage and automate every element of Exchange
   Server 2013 with PowerShell such as mailboxes,
   distribution groups, and address lists

Please check **www.PacktPub.com** for information on our titles

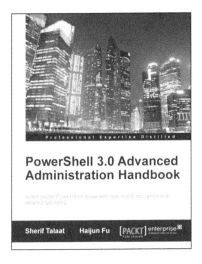

PowerShell 3.0 Advanced Administration Handbook

ISBN: 978-1-84968-642-6   Paperback: 370 pages

A fast-paced PowerShell guide with real-world scenarios and detailed solutions

1. Discover and understand the concept of Windows PowerShell 3.0

2. Learn the advanced topics and techniques for a professional PowerShell scripting

3. Explore the secret of building custom PowerShell snap-ins and modules

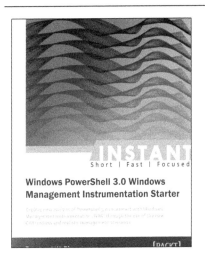

Instant Windows Powershell 3.0 Windows Management Instrumentation Starter [Instant]

ISBN: 978-1-84968-962-5   Paperback: 66 pages

Explore new abilities of PowerShell 3.0 to interact with Windows Management Instrumentation (WMI) through the use of the new CIM cmdlets and realistic management scenarios

1. Learn something new in an Instant! A short, fast, focused guide delivering immediate results.

2. Create CIM sessions to local and remote systems

3. Execute WMI queries using Windows Remote Management

Please check **www.PacktPub.com** for information on our titles

www.ingramcontent.com/pod-product-compliance
Lightning Source LLC
LaVergne TN
LVHW080105070326

832902LV00014B/2441